ASHLAND

The Story of Zacchaeus

Written by
Marty Rhodes Figley
Illustrated by
Cat Bowman Smith

WILLIAM B. EERDMANS PUBLISHING COMPANY
Grand Rapids, Michigan

For Keith LaFrance Figley, the writer —M.R.F.

To Kathryn, Bob, Mary, Jim, Cheryl, and Bill —C.B.S.

© 1995 Wm. B. Eerdmans Publishing Co.
255 Jefferson Ave. S.E., Grand Rapids, Michigan 49503

Printed in Hong Kong

00 99 98 97 96 95   7 6 5 4 3 2 1

Library of Congress Cataloging-in-Publication Data

Figley, Marty Rhodes, 1948-
   The story of Zacchaeus / written by Marty Rhodes Figley;
illustrated by Cat Bowman Smith.
    p.   cm.
  ISBN 0-8028-5092-8 (alk. paper)
  1. Zacchaeus (Biblical character) — Juvenile literature. 2. Bible. N.T.
— Biography — Juvenile literature. 3. Bible stories. English — N.T.
[1. Zacchaeus (Biblical character) 2. Bible stories. — N.T.]
I. Smith, Cat Bowman, ill. II. Title.
BS2520.Z3F54   1995
226.4'092 — dc20   94-46174
                                         CIP
                                          AC

Zacchaeus
was not a nice man.

He was so mean he would grab candy
from a baby if he was hungry.
Or take an old man's jacket if he felt cold.
Sometimes he would forget to feed his pet bird.

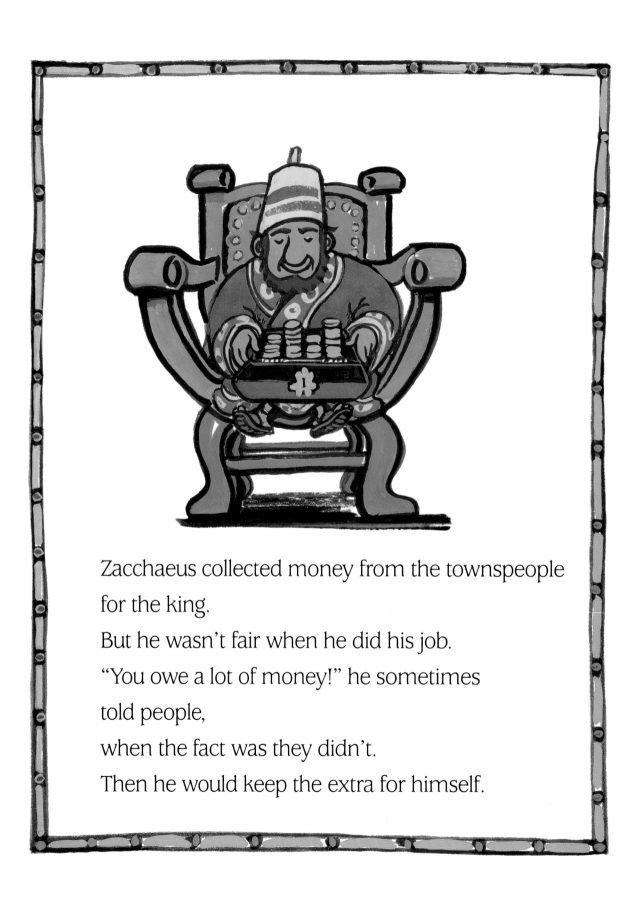

Zacchaeus collected money from the townspeople
for the king.
But he wasn't fair when he did his job.
"You owe a lot of money!" he sometimes
told people,
when the fact was they didn't.
Then he would keep the extra for himself.

Zacchaeus had become a very rich man.

He had large piles of gold,

and large piles of silver.

He lived in a big house,

ate lots of good food,

and wore fancy clothes.

He thought these things would impress people.

But nobody liked him.

When Zaccheus walked down the street,
the townspeople would cross to the other side.
"That Zaccheus is not a nice man,"
they would mutter.
Babies would cry. Dogs would growl.

Zacchaeus didn't have a single friend,
not a single visitor to his big house.
This made him sad—
but not sad enough to change his ways.
Zacchaeus liked having lots of money.

A tall man Zacchaeus was not. In fact, he was very short.
He had to have his clothes cut down to his small size.
He had to stand on a stool to reach things on the top shelf.
And sometimes Zacchaeus got lost in a crowd.

One day Zacchaeus got caught up in a very big crowd. They had gathered for an important event—Jesus was coming to town! How exciting! Everyone was happy. Zacchaeus wanted to see Jesus too. But, as usual, he was lost in the crowd. "If only I had my stool," he thought.

Zacchaeus raced to
his big house,
found his stool
in the kitchen,
and lugged it back
to the crowd.
But it wasn't
high enough.

Then he spied a house with a tall porch.
"I'll climb to the top step," Zacchaeus thought.
"Then I'll be able to see all around."
But all he could see was the backs of
people's heads.

"I've got it!" exclaimed Zacchaeus.
"I'll climb a tree!"

First he tried climbing a willow tree.

But the branches were too limber.

They bent and swayed and dropped him on the ground.

Then he tried climbing a palm tree. But the trunk was so slick he slid down and hit the ground with a thud.

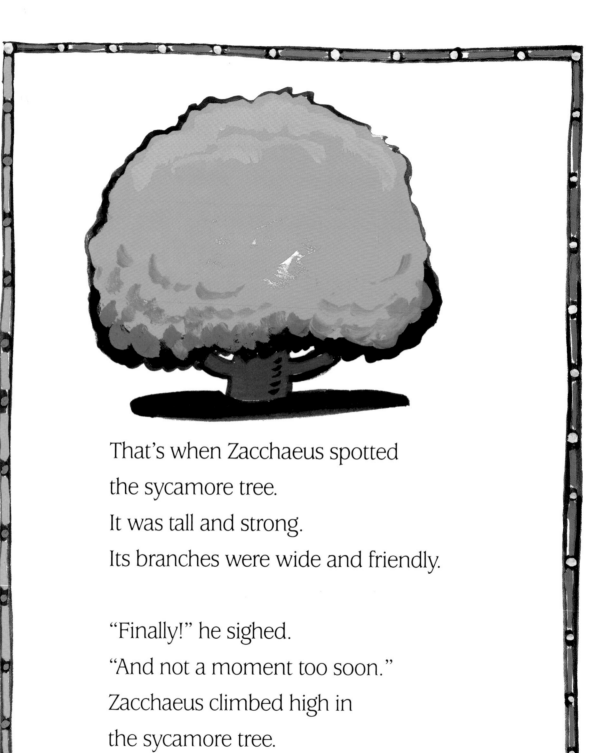

That's when Zacchaeus spotted
the sycamore tree.
It was tall and strong.
Its branches were wide and friendly.

"Finally!" he sighed.
"And not a moment too soon."
Zacchaeus climbed high in
the sycamore tree.
Now he could see all around him.

At last
Jesus arrived.
The crowd
was happy.
Even Zacchaeus
was happy.

As Jesus moved through the crowd, people
pressed close to him, wanting to be near
him, wanting to spend time with him.

When Jesus reached the sycamore tree,
he looked straight up—at Zacchaeus!
"Zacchaeus, come down," he called.
"W-W-Who, me?" Zacchaeus stammered.
"Yes, you—climb down, and hurry,"
Jesus answered.
"I want to stay at your house today."

The crowd couldn't
believe what their ears were hearing.
"Why does Jesus want to stay with him?"
they muttered.
"That Zacchaeus is not a nice man."

But Jesus smiled kindly at Zacchaeus.
Zacchaeus scrambled down from the sycamore
and took Jesus to his big house.
At last he would have a visitor!

Jesus talked to Zacchaeus like a friend,
not like a little man, not like a bad man.
Jesus' love made Zacchaeus see things
more clearly. It was like sitting
in the sycamore tree.

"I will change my ways for you, Jesus," he said.

"I will give half my gold and silver to the poor.

I will try my best to be a nice man.

I will remember to feed my pet bird."

Jesus nodded and hugged Zacchaeus.

"I am pleased," he said.

Ever since that special day,
Zacchaeus has been
a different man—
kind, fair, and
happy.

When he walks down the street,
the townspeople greet him.
"That Zacchaeus is a good man,"
they say to themselves.
Babies smile.
Dogs lick his hand.

Now Zacchaeus has lots of friends,
lots of visitors to his big house.
And a very fat pet bird.